MICROWAVE OVEN COOKBOOK

THIS BOOK BELONGS TO

_____
_____
_____

TABLE OF CONTENTS

1. Chocolate Chip Cookie in a Cup
2. 10-MINUTE GLUTEN-FREE ENCHILADAS
3. Microwave English Muffin
4. Microwave Egg Breakfast Sandwich
5. Microwave Granola
6. Microwave Ropa Vieja
7. Coffee Mug Cake
8. Two Minute Scrambled Eggs
9. Microwave Ratatouille
10. Cinnamon Roll Mug Cake
11. Macaroni and Cheese in a Mug
12. Microwave Baked Potatoes
13. Microwave Monkey Bread
14. SUPER EASY CHICKEN PENNE & TOMATOES
15. Microwave Apples with Cinnamon
16. Microwave Chocolate Fudge
17. Microwave Gajar Ka Halwa
18. Microwave Machchli Lal Masala
19. Microwave Caramel Custard
20. Microwave Dhokla Recipe
21. Microwave Paneer Tikka Recipe
22. Microwave Chocolate Cake Recipe
23. Microwave Eggless Cookies
24. Two Minute Brownie
25. Microwave Hazelnut Cake
26. Microwave Besan Kati Pindi
27. Microwave Gobhi Dahiwala
28. Microwave Hazelnut Cake
29. Spaghetti Squash Alfredo
30. Beat-the-Clock Chili
31. Ginger-Soy Steamed Cod

32. Banana Bread Mug Cake
33. Shrimp Tacos
34. Easy Pea Risotto
35. Homemade Microwave Popcorn
36. Microwave Polenta
37. Cookie Dough Microwave Oatmeal
38. 5 Minute Microwave Cornbread
39. Micro-Poached Salmon
40. Single-Serve Chocolate Mug Cake
41. Poached Pears with Ruby-Red Raspberry Sauce
42. Microwave Mug Chocolate Cake
43. Microwave Oatmeal Bars
44. Honey-Lemon Chicken Enchiladas
45. 15-Minute Meat Loaf
46. Fruit & Granola Crisp with Yogurt
47. Microwave Egg Sandwich
48. Zucchini Ham Frittata
49. Microwave Parmesan Chicken
50. Cod Delight
51. Dressed-Up Meatballs
52. Breakfast Potatoes
53. Sandwiches with Mashed Potatoes
54. Salmon with Tarragon Sauce
55. Minted Beet Salad
56. Coconut Acorn Squash
57. Microwave Beef & Cheese Enchiladas
58. Quick Poached Salmon with Cucumber Sauce
59. Microwave Chicken Kiev
60. Chipotle Ranch Chicken Tacos
61. Italian Chicken Cordon Bleu
62. Mini Burgers with the Works
63. Super-Stuffed Mexican Potatoes
64. Turkey Enchilada Stack

65. Granola Cereal Bars
66. Chicken and Rice Soup Mix
67. Bart's Black Bean Soup for Two
68. Instant Mac & Cheese in a Mug
69. Quick Egg, Mushroom & Ham Cup
70. EGG FRIED RICE IN A MUG
71. 1-minute Microwave Quiche in a Mug
72. Homemade Single-Serve Microwave Spaghetti
73. SPINACH RICOTTA LASAGNA IN A MUG
74. PIZZA MUG CAKE
75. Hasty Chocolate Pudding
76. Potato Chips
77. Microwave Baked Potato
78. Chili Cheese Dip V
79. Southwest Chicken Casserole
80. Microwave Oven Peanut Brittle
81. Shelby's Microwave Meat Loaf
82. Microwave Loin of Pork
83. Basic Microwave Risotto
84. Gourmet Microwave Popcorn
85. Microwave Chocolate Mug Cake
86. Microwave Corn on the Cob

Chocolate Chip Cookie in a Cup

Prep Time 5 mins

Cook Time 1 min

Total Time 6 mins

Servings: 1

Ingredients

- 1 tbsp Butter
- 1 tsp Sugar (granulated)
- 1 Tablespoon Dark Brown Sugar
- 3 tsp Vanilla Extract
- Kosher Salt
- 1 Egg Yolk Save the egg white for another dish
- Scant 1/4 cup All Purpose Flour
- 2 tbsp Semi Sweet Chocolate Chips plus extra for sprinkle

Instructions

1. Microwave your butter to soften it. Butter should not be boiled.
2. vanilla, and salt Mix well.
3. Add the yolk just to your cup. Mix well.
4. Remix with flour. 1/4 cup all-purpose flour, little less than full.
5. Stir in the chocolate chips. It should now resemble cookie dough. Sprinkle the cookie batter with chocolate chips.
6. Microwave for 40-60 seconds, checking after 40 seconds. Mine is 50 sec. Like a conventional cookie, this will continue to cook as it cools. If it's dry or cakey, try less time.
7. Serve

10-MINUTE GLUTEN-FREE ENCHILADAS

Yield: SERVES 4-6

Prep time: 5 MINUTES

Cook time: 5 MINUTES

Total time: 10 MINUTES

INGREDIENTS

- 1 (15 oz) can gluten free enchilada sauce 12 GF corn tortillas
- 2 Cups of cooked chicken, shredded
- 1 cup shredded cheese (cheddar, Monterey jack, Colby, etc.)
- optional, cilantro, beans, corn.

INSTRUCTIONS

1. Wrap your gluten-free corn tortillas in a paper towel and microwave for 30 seconds to soften them.

2. Cover the bottom of a microwave-safe rectangular casserole dish with approximately 12 cup enchilada sauce.

3. Combine the chicken, any preferred filling ingredients, and about 1 cup of enchilada sauce in a mixing bowl.

4. Drizzle the remaining enchilada sauce over each tortilla. Roll each tortilla with 2 12-3 Tablespoons of filling. Repeat with the remaining tortillas and filling in the pan, seam side down.

5. Drizzle any remaining enchilada sauce over the enchiladas. Top with the shredded cheese.

6. Microwave for 5-7 minutes, or until the cheese is melted and the sauce is boiling.

Microwave English Muffin

Servings: 1

Ingredients

- 2 tbsp peanut flour
- 1/2 tsp baking powder
- 2 tbsp unsweetened canned
- 1 big egg replaces 2 large egg whites
- 1-2 tbsp liquid I used milk
- Cinnamon
- Salt
- Optional sugar/sweetener for a sweet version
- Gluten free dusting flour (optional)

For the Paleo option

- 2 tbsp almond flour
- 1/2 tsp baking powder
- 2 tbsp unsweetened canned
- 1 Large Eggs / 2 Egg White
- 1-2 tbsp liquid Almond milk
- Cinnamon
- Salt
- Choisir de l'édul Optional sweetener

For the Vegan option

- 2 tbsp peanut flour
- 2 tsp baking powder
- 2 tbsp unsweetened canned
- 1 flax eggs
- 1 tsp flaxseed meal
- 3 tsp water
- 1-2 tbsp liquid Almond milk
- Cinnamon

Instructions

1. Add peanut flour and baking powder to a microwave-safe cereal dish and stir well.
2. Add the canned pumpkin and 2 egg whites or 1 egg and mix well. Add desired milk/liquid.
3. Microwave for 2-4 minutes with cinnamon and sea salt, depending on power.
4. Remove from microwave and liberally flour both sides. Let cool, then slice in half and toast. Like an English muffin

For the oven option

Preheat oven to 350°F and bake for 12-15 minutes, until golden brown on top and a toothpick inserted comes out clean. Mine takes 12 minutes and I oil the bowl thoroughly to remove it gently.

Microwave Egg Breakfast Sandwich

Prep Time5 minutes

Total Time5 minutes

Servings1

Ingredients

- 1 Everything bagel
- 3/4 c. egg whites
- 10-15 green chard leaves
- 1wedges Herb & Garlic Cheese
- 2 tomato slices
- 2-4 avocado slices
- salt kosher
- Hot sauce Cholula

Instructions

1. Toast the bagel thinly. Whisk the egg whites in a small dish with the spinach leaves and kosher salt. Microwave on HIGH for 1 minute 30 seconds, watching out for overflowing eggs.

2. Top the toasted bagel with a cheese wedge and tomato slices. Place the cooked egg on top of the cheese, tomato, and avocado. If desired, add extra salt and spicy sauce.

Microwave Granola

- 1/2 c. butter
- 3/4 c. brown sugar
- 1/4 honey
- 1/4 water
- 1/4 tsp salt
- Cinnamon, 1/2 tsp
- 3 cups oats
- 1 c. bran flakes
- 1 c. peanuts (I use cashews)
- 1 c wheat germ 1 (I accidentally left this out)
- 1 c. sunflowers seeds
- 1/2 coconut (I used shaved)
- 1 cup sliced almonds (I used 1/4 cup almonds and 3/4 cup pecans)
- 1 cup raisins, craisins.

Pour the ingredients into a large glass basin.

Microwave for 8 minutes on high, stirring halfway.

Other ingredients except dried fruit

Microwave for 4 minutes on high, stirring halfway. Golden granola is best.

Gently fold in dried fruit if desired.

Cool on a baking sheet, stirring periodically to avoid clumps.

Keep airtight.

Microwave Ropa Vieja

Total: 1 hr 10 min

Prep: 10 min

Inactive: 10 min

Cook: 50 min

Yield: 4 servings

Ingredients

1. 1/4 inch onion, sliced
2. 3 minced garlic cloves
3. 1 tsp cumin
4. 1/4 tsp dried oregano
5. 2 tbsp extra virgin olive
6. SALT AND PEPPER
7. 14 oz. crushed tomatoes
8. 1/2 cup sliced roasted red peppers in jar
9. 2 tsp soy sauce
10. 1 dried bay leaf
11. 1 1/4 lb flank steak, sliced into 3 1/2-inch strips
12. 1/3 cup half pimento-stuffed olives
13. 3 tbsp fresh cilantro leaves, chopped
14. Serving rice

Directions

1. 1/2 Tbsp salt & a few grinds of black pepper in a microwave-safe 4-quart bowl Cover the bowl with plastic wrap and a paring knife incision in the center to release excess steam. Microwave on high for 4 minutes, or until

the onions are tender and transparent. A 30-second increment if the onions aren't cooked through. (Be cautious when removing the plastic wrap.)
2. Tomatoes red peppers soy sauce bay leaf 1/2 teaspoon salt and pepper Stir in the meat. Cover the bowl with 2 plastic wrap sheets, slitting the middle. Microwave on high (100%) for 20 minutes. Remove the plastic wrap, mix, and re-cover. Microwave for 20 minutes on high (at full power). Uncover and cool for 5 minutes.
3. Transfer the steak to a chopping board. (It won't be fall-apart delicate yet but should shred.) Return the steak to the dish and toss in the olives. Cover the bowl with plastic wrap, slice the middle and microwave for 5 minutes at 100% power. Cover the ropa vieja for 5 minutes. Serve with cilantro rice.

Coffee Mug Cake

Prep Time4 minutes

Cook Time1 minute

Total Time5 minutes

Yield1 mug cake

Ingredients

- 3 tbsp oat or almond flour
- 1/4 tsp baking powder
- 1/16 Tsp Salt
- 1 tsp sugar
- In the case of almond flour, use 1 egg or 2 tbsp water.
- 2 tsp oil (or applesauce)
- 1/4 tsp vanilla

For The Streusel

- 1/8 tsp Cinnamon
- 1 1/4 tsp streusel
- 1/4 to 1/2 tablespoon oil, butter, or applesauce (low-fat)

- tiny salt
- 2 walnut halves

Instructions

I like the oil or buttery spread since I dislike fat-free baked products. Preheat oven to 330 F. Mix thoroughly the dry ingredients. Mix in the wet until smooth. Mix streusel ingredients in a small bowl. Half-fill a greased muffin tin (or use a ramekin or mug, if using the microwave). Pour remaining batter over streusel. Finish with the remaining streusel. Bake for 12-13 minutes or microwave for 1 minute. Microwave timings vary with wattage.

Two Minute Scrambled Eggs

Ingredients:

- 2 egg
- 2 tbsp milk
- 2 tbsp. shredded cheese
- salt, pepper, and herbs

Directions:

Spray a 12 oz. microwave-safe coffee cup or other dish. Beat in eggs and milk.

45 seconds on HIGH; stir.

Microwave for 30–45 seconds more to almost set eggs.

Add cheese, salt, pepper, and herbs.

Microwave Ratatouille

Total: 30 min

Prep: 10 min

Cook: 20 min

Yield: 4 servings

Ingredients

- 1 medium yellow onion, sliced 1/4"
- 2 minced garlic cloves
- 3 chopped sun-dried tomatoes
- 1/4 cup olive oil
- 1 tsp chopped thyme (from about 3 sprigs)
- SALT AND PEPPER
- 1 small eggplant, peeled and sliced into 1/4-inch rounds (about 6 ounces)
- 1 small zucchini, cut 1/4" thick (about 4 ounces)
- 1 yellow squash, cut 1/4"
- 2 plum tomatoes, sliced 1/4 inch thick (about 8 ounces)

Directions

1. In a microwave-safe 9-inch pie dish, combine the onion, garlic, sun-dried tomatoes, 1 tablespoon olive oil, 1/2 teaspoon thyme, 1/2 teaspoon salt, and pepper. Cover with wax paper. 7 minutes in a 1, 100 watt microwave or 10 minutes in a 700 watt microwave until the onions are tender and transparent. If the onions are still raw, microwave covered for 30 seconds more.
2. Cooked onions are tossed with 2 tablespoons of the remaining olive oil, 1/2 teaspoon thyme, 1/2 teaspoon salt, and some black pepper in a large bowl. Gently toss in the plum tomato slices.
3. Lay shingle pieces in a circle over the sautéed onions in the pie plate. Lightly salt the dish. Wrap with wax paper. 9 minutes in a 1100 watt microwave or 14 minutes in a 700 watt microwave until the veggies are tender. If the veggies still have resistance when pierced with a paring knife, microwave covered for 30 seconds more. To remove excess moisture, microwave uncovered for 3 minutes (1100 watts) or 4 minutes

(700 watts) on high (100 percent power). Drizzle with remaining olive oil.

Cinnamon Roll Mug Cake

Servings: 1 Serving

Prep5 minutes

Cook1 minute

Ready in: 6 minutes

Ingredients

- Applesauce 2 tbsp
- 1 tbsp oil
- 1 tsp buttermilk
- 1/4 tsp vanilla
- 1/4 cup flour
- 2.5 tsp light brown sugar
- 3/4 tsp cinnamon
- 1 nutmeg, ground (optional)
- 1/4 tsp baking powder
- 1/8 tsp salt
- 1 Recipe Recipe for Cream Cheese Icing
- cream cheese icing
- 1 tbsp softened cream cheese
- 2 tbsp sugar powder
- 1 tbsp milk

Instructions

1. Prepare Cream Cheese Icing as directed. In a mug, mix all ingredients (except Cream Cheese Icing) and whisk with a fork until nearly smooth.

2. Microwave mixture for 1 minute on high power, then check cake. Microwave for 15 seconds more if not fully done. Warm with Cream Cheese Icing.

Macaroni and Cheese in a Mug

Prep Time 5 minutes

Cook Time 10 minutes

Total Time 15 minutes

Ingredients

Whole grain elbow macaroni

Water

Cheddar-Jack Shredded Cheese

Splash of milk

Instructions

1. In a large microwave-safe mug or bowl, combine 1/3 cup whole grain elbow macaroni and 1/3 cup + 1/4 cup water. Microwave for 6 minutes, stirring every 4 minutes.

2. (Microwave periods may vary based on microwave intensity. I think my is average. If you have a powerful microwave, check it after 1 minute to make sure it hasn't dried up.

3. The pasta should be cooked with a thin layer of pasta water at the bottom. Let it go.

4. 1 cup shredded Cheddar Jack cheese (pictured above). Microwave for 30–45 seconds to melt cheese.

5. Add a splash of milk and mix thoroughly (maybe 2 teaspoons).

Microwave Baked Potatoes

Prep Time 2 mins

Cook Time 20 mins

Total Time 22 mins

Servings: 4

Ingredients

- 4 potatoes Russet
- a microwave
- whatever baked potato toppings you desire

Instructions

1. Wash potatoes well.

2. Poke them with a fork (this is optional, but makes me feel better)

3. Microwave without a container. You don't have to put them on a paper towel.

4. Cook for 10 minutes on high.

5. Each potato (careful it will be hot)

6. Cook for 10 minutes on high.

7. They should be soft to the touch when done. With 4 huge ones, 20 minutes was sufficient. Depending on the number of potatoes, you may need to adjust the cooking time.

Microwave Monkey Bread

What you Need

- 7 tbsp. butter
- 2/3 c sugar

- vanilla 1 tsp
- 2 tsp cinnamon
- 2 cans biscuits

Sugar, vanilla, and cinnamon melted butter Pour sugar mixture over biscuits. Coat well.

4 minutes on high Allow 2 minutes to cool. Serve on a platter.

SUPER EASY CHICKEN PENNE & TOMATOES

Yield: 8 SERVINGS

INGREDIENTS

- 4 peeled garlic cloves
- 2 cup cherry tomatoes
- 3 c uncooked penne
- 3chicken broth + 1 cup white wine = 4 c.
- 1/2 tsp salt, finely ground pepper
- 2 tsp dried basil
- 2 cup mozzarella cheese
- 2 c. Cubed grilled chicken

INSTRUCTIONS

1. Olive oil Deep Covered Baker
2. Add the minced garlic to the dish.
3. Tomatoes Microwave on HIGH for 4-5 minutes, stirring every 2 minutes, until tomatoes burst.
4. Crush tomatoes with a spoon.
1. Add pasta, broth and salt and pepper.

5. Microwave covered baker (or casserole dish) on HIGH 16-18 minutes or until pasta is cooked, stirring every 10 minutes.
6. Carefully remove baker and lift away from you.
7. Combine cheese and chicken in baker. Mix in basil.

Microwave Apples with Cinnamon

Yield: 1 serving

Prep Time3 minutes

Cook Time2 minutes

Total Time5 minutes

Ingredients

- 1 apple
- 1 sweetener packet
- 1/4 tsp cinnamon
- 1/4 t cornstarch
- 1 tbsp water

Instructions

Peel, core, and slice or dice an apple. Place in a freezer-safe plastic bag with the rest of the ingredients.

Seal the plastic bag and shake well. In a small microwave-safe bowl, combine all ingredients and cover loosely.

Gently reopen bag to vent. 2-minute microwavable on high, longer for large apples.

Carefully open bag and pour over pita chips, flour tortilla chips, oats, or ice cream.

Microwave Chocolate Fudge

Total Cook Time 30 mins

Prep Time 10 mins

Cook Time 20 mins

Servings 5

Ingredients

- 3/4 c. semi-sweet chocolate chips
- 14 oz sweetened condensed milk
- 1 tbsp. butter
- 2 tsp chopped walnuts (optional)

Chocolate Fudge

1. Microwave chocolate chips, sweetened condensed milk, and butter or margarine. Microwave on medium for 3-5 minutes, swirling once or twice, until chips are melted.

2. If desired, add nuts.

3. Pour into a well-greased pan.

4. Set in the fridge.

Microwave Gajar Ka Halwa

Servings: 6

Prep Time: 10 mins

Cook Time: 30 mins

Total Cook Time: 40 mins

Ingredients

- 1 kilogram grated carrots
- 1 can condensed milk

- 1 tsp powdered green cardamom
- 5-6 blanched and shredded almonds
- 8-10 raisin
- 2 tsp ghee
- Microwave 1200 W

Microwave Gajar Ka Halwa

1. Fill a dish with carrots and condensed milk. Cover and simmer on High for 5 minutes.
2. Cook for 10 minutes with 50% cover, stirring twice.
3. The carrots will start to look somewhat shiny and the moisture will have gone.
4. Cook the cardamom, ghee, half the almonds and raisins for a minute on Hi.

Microwave Machchli Lal Masala

Total Cook Time 1 hr 15 mins

Prep Time 15 mins

Cook Time 1 hr

Recipe Servings 4

Ingredients

Marinate together:

- 500 g Fish
- 1 tbsp Lemon

Grind together:

- 2-3 red chilies (soaked in vinegar for 1 hour)
- 2 tsp Vinegar
- 2 tsp Bhuna channa
- Garlic, 1 tbsp.

- 1/4 cup onion, chopped
- 1/2 tsp Salt
- 4 thyme
- 2 peppercorns
- 1 tsp Cinnamon (broken to small pieces)
- 1/2 javitri

For garnishing Mint leaves

Microwave Machchli Lal Masala

1. Marinate the fish for an hour in the paste.
2. a saucer-plate in a dish
3. Lay the fillets on top, thicker portions outward.
4. Cook uncovered at HI for 8 minutes, rotating once.
5. Brush with oil if desired, but prevent.
6. Serve fillets on a serving plate with mint leaves.

Microwave Caramel Custard

Servings: 6

Prep Time: 05 mins

Cook Time: 20 mins

Total Cook Time: 25 mins

Ingredients

- 3/4 cup Sugar
- 2 tbsp.water
- 4 Eggs
- Cornflour 2 tsp
- 2 cups Milk
- Vanilla Essence 1 tsp

Microwave Caramel Custard

1. Cook uncovered at HI 2 minutes with 1/4 cup sugar and water. Stir thoroughly and simmer, uncovered, for 3-4 minutes or until a dark brown color. Set aside
2. Then add the vanilla and sugar. Add the milk slowly, beating constantly.
3. Cook covered at 30% for 10-12 minutes, rotating the pan halfway through.
4. Let cool, then serve. After a few tries, you may need to modify the timing.

Microwave Dhokla Recipe

Total Cook Time15 mins

Prep Time05 mins

Cook Time10 mins

Recipe Servings10

Ingredients

- Microwave 1200 W
- 1 c besan
- Ginger Paste 1 tsp
- Paste de chilli
- Salt and turmeric tsp
- 1 t sugar
- 1 tsp oil
- 1 c sour curds
- 1 c water
- 1 tsp salt

For the tad ka:

- 1 tsp rai
- 4-5 Kati patta
- Julienne 2-3 green chillies

- 1 tsp Oil

For garnishing:

Dhania

Coconut

How to Make

1. Combine besan, ginger, chilli paste, salt, turmeric, sugar, and oil. Until smooth.
2. Remix in the water.
3. Pour into a greased microwaveable dish, cover, and heat at HI for 6-8 minutes, turning the dish once.
4. Heat the tad ka oil and add the rai and Kathy patta. Add 1 cup water after a minute of browning.
5. Tad ka over the cut dhokla. Serve with dhania and coconut.

Microwave Paneer Tikka

Recipe Servings: 4

Prep Time: 02 mins

Cook Time: 40 mins

Total Cook Time: 42 mins

Ingredients

- 1 kg paneer cubes 1.5"
- 2 tbsp paste
- Ginger Paste 2 tsp
- 1 tsp masala
- 2 tsp chilli powder
- 1 tsp powdered black pepper
- Salt, 1 tbs

- A few crimson droplets
- 3 tsp vinegar
- Brushing oil
- 1 Lemon (quartered)
- 1 onion

How to Make

1. Stir in the masalas and let aside for 20-30 minutes.
2. In a larger dish, place a greased saucer plate.
3. Cook uncovered on HI for 4 minutes with paneer along the edge.
4. Turn over, brush with oil, and cook for 4 minutes on HI.

Microwave Chocolate Cake

Total Cook Time 40 mins

Prep Time 10 mins

Cook Time 30 mins

Recipe Servings 4

Ingredients

- 2 cup maida
- 1 3/4 cup castor sugar
- 2/3 cup fat (butter, oil)
- 2/3 cup cocoa powder
- 1 c water
- Vanilla essence 1 tsp
- Baking soda 1.5 tsp
- Baking powder, 1/2 tbsp
- 1 tsp salt
- 3 eggs

How to Make

1. Line the pans with butter paper or oil and sprinkle with maida or sugar.
2. Flour, cocoa, baking powder, baking soda
3. Seasoning the meat with salt, sugar, oil, Beat the ingredients with a wooden spoon or a beater.
4. Add the eggs one at a time, beating until smooth. When done, the batter should be shiny.
5. Pour the batter into each dish.
6. Bake each cake for 2 minutes at combi 3. Bake for 2 minutes after rotating container.
7. Revolute and bake 1 minute. Remove cake from pan after 5 minutes.

Microwave Eggless Cookies

Total Cook Time 25 mins

Prep Time 10 mins

Cook Time 15 mins

Recipe Servings 2

Ingredients

- 1.5 cup flour
- Milk, 1/4 c.
- 1 tsp vinegar
- 1 c. Butter
- 1/2 cup powdered sugar
- Vanilla essence 1 tsp

How to Make

Combine flour, vinegar, butter, sugar, and vanilla.

Make a smooth dough with flour.

Flatten 24 tiny balls using a fork.

Microwave six cookies at a time on a greaseproof paper-lined baking pan for 1 1/2 - 2 1/4 minutes, depending on their size.

Half-turn the tray halfway through cooking.

Chill on a wire rack.

Pour the remaining mixture.

Turn on the grill according your oven's instructions.

Two Minute Brownie

Total Cook Time07 mins

Prep Time05 mins

Cook Time02 mins

Recipe Servings2

Ingredients

- 2 tbsp flour
- 2 tbsp powdered sugar
- 2 tsp cocoa powder
- 2 tsp milk
- 1 tbsp oil

How to Make

1.Microwave-safe cup

2.Stuff it with the dry goods.

3.Add the wet ingredients.

4Microwave for a few seconds. (Microwave settings vary.)

5.Top your cup cake with your favorite ice cream.

Microwave Hazelnut Cake

Total Cook Time 20 mins

Prep Time 05 mins

Cook Time 15 mins

Recipe Servings 4

Ingredients

- 1 cup maida/flour
- 1/2 c powdered sugar
- Baking powder 1 tbs
- 1/2 cup raw oil
- 1/2 cup hazelnut
- 1 egg (whisked)

How to Make

1. Microwave baking powder, maida, and sugar.
2. An egg in another bowl. Add nutella and oil. Whisk in the nutella.
3. Mix the egg mixture into the dry ingredients bowl. For a thinner mixture, add 2-3 tablespoons cold milk.
4. Microwave the bowl for 2-3 minutes on HIGH.

Microwave Besan Kathy Pindi

Recipe Servings: 4

Prep Time: 10 mins

Cook Time: 45 mins

Total Cook Time: 55 mins

Ingredients

- 3/4 cup basin
- 1 tsp turmeric
- 1/4 tsp Asafoetida
- 2 tsp salt
- 1 tsp south
- 2 c yogurt (preferably hung)
- 6 c water
- 1 tsp oil
- 1 tbsp seed
- 1 tsp fenugreek seed
- Ajwain, 2 tsp
- 4 bad is
- 4 cup chopped mixed veggies

For garnishing:

Coriander leaves

How to Make

1. Add salt, pepper, and south to basin mixture.
2. Mix in yoghurt to make a paste
3. Now add the remainder.
4. Add 6 cups water.
5. Pour the bad is into a deep dish and add the oil.
6. Cook covered for 3 minutes, stirring once.
7. Cook covered on high heat for 10 minutes, stirring once.
8. Cook covered for 20 minutes at 70% power, stirring twice.
9. Add coriander and serve hot.

Microwave Gobhi Dahiwala

Recipe Servings: 2

Prep Time: 20 mins

Cook Time: 25 mins

Total Cook Time: 45 mins

Ingredients

- 500 g cauliflower
- 1 tsp Ghee
- 2 tsp cumin
- A pinch Asafoetida
- Yogurt, 1/4 cup
- 1 tbsp chopped ginger
- 1 tbsp coriander seeds
- 2 t salt
- 1/2 tsp turmeric
- 1/4 t garam masala
- 1 tbsp coarsely chopped green chilies

For garnishing:

- 2 tsp cumin seeds, toasted
- 2 tsp coriander leaves

How to Make

1. Cook ghee, cumin, and asafoetida covered on HI for 2 minutes.

2. Mix in ginger and yoghurt until smooth.

3. Cook at 70% for 2 minutes. Soup is ready when it smells like coriander!

4. Mix in the cauliflower. 12 minutes covered at 70%, stirring once.

5. Cook it longer for softer.

6. Garnish with cumin powder and coriander leaves.

Microwave Hazelnut Cake

Total Cook Time 20 mins

Prep Time 05 mins

Cook Time 15 mins

Recipe Servings 4

Ingredients

- 1 cup maida/flour
- 1/2 c powdered sugar
- baking powder 1 tbs
- 1/2 CUP RAW OIL
- 1/2 CUP hazelnut
- 1 Egg (whisked)

How to Make

1. Microwave baking powder, maida, and sugar.
2. An egg in another bowl. Add nutella and oil. Whisk in the nutella.
3. Mix the egg mixture into the dry ingredients bowl. For a thinner mixture, add 2-3 tablespoons cold milk.
4. Microwave the bowl for 2-3 minutes on HIGH.

Spaghetti Squash Alfredo

YIELDS: 4

Ingredients

- Squash, 4 pound
- 2 tsp salt
- 1/4 tsp pepper
- 1 C. HALF&HALF
- 3 tsp butter
- 1 c. Parmesan

- 4 cup shredded Mozzarella

Directions

1. Remove seeds from spaghetti squash halves. Prick outsides with a sharp knife; salt and pepper insides with 1/4 teaspoon each. Microwave on high for 10 minutes, cut sides down, until soft.
2. Meanwhile, heat half-and-half and butter over medium heat for 5 minutes, or until slightly reduced, then whisk in finely grated Parmesan cheese. Divide sauce among squash halves and top with 2 tablespoons shredded mozzarella cheese. Broil for 1–2 minutes until bubbling and golden. Optional: With a green salad.

Beat-the-Clock Chili

YIELDS: 4

TOTAL TIME: 24 mins

Ingredients

- 1 yellow pepper
- 1 no-salt added can tomato dice
- kidney beans, 1 can
- 11/4 pound 90% lean ground beef
- 4 flour tortillas
- 1 bundle green onions
- Chili powder, 2 tbsp
- Tomato paste, 1 tbsp
- 1 1/2 tsp cumin
- 1/2 tsp sugar
- salt
- Fresh cilantro leaves, 1/2 c.
- 8 tsp low-fat sour cream (optional)

Directions

1. Microwave for 1 minute at a time until heated through. Microwave 5 minutes on high with vented plastic wrap. Drain excess liquid and chunk meat with a spoon. Microwave covered for 3 minutes on high; drain liquid.
2. Heat toaster oven to 425 F. 5 minutes in foil-wrapped tortillas.
3. Add green onions, chili powder, tomato paste, cumin, sugar, and 1/2 teaspoon salt to meat mixture. Microwave on High for 4 minutes. Add cilantro.
4. Pour chili into 4 bowls and garnish with 2 tablespoons sour cream, if desired, and cilantro leaves. With tortillas

Ginger-Soy Steamed Cod

YIELDS: 4 servings

PREP TIME: 15 mins

TOTAL TIME: 35 mins

Ingredients

- 1 bok choy
- 1 garlic clove
- 4 onions
- 1 tsp sesame oil
- 2 tbsp. soy sauce
- 1 tbsp. rice vinegar
- 2 tsp grated fresh ginger
- 4 skinless, boneless cod fillet
- 2 pkg precooked brown rice

Directions

1. 1-inch-long chunks of bok choy Rinse with cold water, swishing to remove sand. Move bok choy to colander, sand in basin. Rinse with fresh water as needed. Don't dry spin
2. Choy and half of garlic in a large microwave-safe dish. 4–5 minutes on High until soft. Cover and leave.
3. To make green onions, finely slice the dark-green tops, saving the white and light-green sections for decoration.
4. In a 9-inch glass pie pan, combine green onion and remaining garlic. Microwave on High for 2–3 minutes or until green onions are soft.
5. Top with cod, tucking thin ends of fillet under to form equal thickness. Microwave fish on High for 4–5 minutes, or until barely opaque throughout. Take pie plate out of microwave and cover for 2 minutes.
6. Microwave brown rice as directed.
7. Onion tops and liquid from pie dish are served on top of bok choi. With rice.

Banana Bread Mug Cake

PREP TIME 4 MINUTES

COOK TIME 1 MINUTE

TOTAL TIME 5 MINUTES

SERVINGS 1 SERVING

INGREDIENTS

- 1/3 c. mashed bananas 1 ripe banana, but measure it out
- 1 tbsp oil
- 1 tbsp almond milk
- 1 tbsp natural brown sugar or coconut sugar
- 3 tsp flour or gluten-free flour mix
- pinch salt
- Cinnamon powder

- 1/2 tsp baking powder
- 1 tbsp chopped nuts or chocolate chips

INSTRUCTIONS

1. Then add the milk and sugar. Whisk for 30 seconds to fully mix and crush the banana. Pasteurize the eggs in a large bowl.
2. Stir for 20 seconds more to mix, getting the bottoms as well. Gently fold in nuts and chocolate chips. If you like, top with them.
3. Microwave for 80 seconds. It's acceptable if it's undercooked since it will cook as it cools. It's better undercooked than overdone. Retire and cool for 3 minutes. Belief! Preheat oven to 350F and bake in a 3.5-inch oven-safe ramekin for 25-30 minutes. Remove and cool for 5 minutes. Enjoy with coarse sea salt!

Shrimp Tacos

YIELDS:4

PREP TIME: 10 mins

TOTAL TIME: 30 mins

Ingredients

- 1 tbsp olive oil
- 1 onion
- 1 tiny jalapeo
- 2 c. corn
- 1 c. beans
- 1 lb. deveined medium shrimp
- Lime 2
- 1 avocados
- 1/4 cup cilantro leaves
- 8 flour tortillas

Directions

1. Microwave oil, onion, and jalapeo on High for 4 minutes, stirring once.

2. Microwave corn and beans for 2 minutes on high with vented plastic wrap. Cover and microwave for 3–4 minutes more, or until shrimp are opaque throughout.

3. Make avocado salsa: 2 tbsp lime juice Set aside 8 lime wedges. Lime juice, avocado, and cilantro

4. Microwave 15–20 seconds on High, or until warm, just before serving tacos.

5. Divide shrimp mixture and avocado salsa among tortillas. With lime wedges

Easy Pea Risotto

YIELDS: 4

PREP TIME: 15 mins

TOTAL TIME: 30 mins

Ingredients

- 1 chicken broth
- 2 1/4 c + 2 tbsp water
- 1 Frozen peas pound
- 1 tsp olive oil
- 2 cup Rice (Carnaroli) Arborio
- 1/2 c. grated Parmesan cheese

Directions

1. Warm 2 1/4 cup water and 2 1/4 cup chicken broth in a 2-quart covered pot.

2. Microwave peas and 2 tablespoons water on High for 4 minutes, covered with vented plastic wrap. 1/2 cup peas, 1/4 cup hot broth Cover and purée peas and broth combination. Set aside the peas.
3. Combine olive oil and rice in a 3 1/2–4 quart microwave-safe dish Microwave uncovered on High for 1 minute. Microwave on Medium (50 percent power) for 10 minutes, stirring midway.
4. Cover with vented plastic wrap and cook on Medium for 8 minutes (50 percent power). Add Parmesan, salt, pepper, and remaining peas.
5. To serve, ladle risotto into 4 shallow dishes and top with Parmesan shavings.

Homemade Microwave Popcorn

YIELDS:5 cups

Ingredients

- 1/4 c. popcorn kernels
- 1/2 tsp. canola oil

Directions

1. In a microwave-safe glass dish, combine popcorn and oil.

2. Microwave on high for 3–4 minutes, or until pops are barely 3 seconds apart. Removing the plate To taste.

Microwave Polenta

YIELDS:4

PREP TIME: 5 mins

COOK TIME: 7 mins

TOTAL TIME: 12 mins

Ingredients

- Water, 2 1/4 c.
- 1 cup low-fat milk
- 3/4 c. yellow cornmeal
- 1 1/2 tsp salt

Directions

1. Combine boiling water, milk, cornmeal, and salt in a 2-1/2-quart microwave-safe dish or casserole. Microwave 5 minutes on high, covered with waxed paper.

2. Remove microwave bowl and whisk quickly until smooth (mixture will be lumpy at first). Microwave, covered, on High for 2–3 minutes longer, whisking once. 3 cups

Cookie Dough Microwave Oatmeal

Prep: 5 minutes

Cook: 2 minutes

Total: 7 minutes

YIELD1

INGREDIENTS

- 1/2 cup oats
- 2/3 cup almond milk
- 1/2 tbsp cashew
- 2 tsp maple syrup
- 1/2 tbsp tiny chocolate (for topping)

INSTRUCTIONS

1. Then add unsweetened almond milk and maple syrup to the oats.
2. Microwave for 1 minute on high.
3. Reheat oatmeal and stir. 1 minute more cook Remove and stir.
4. After 2 minutes, sprinkle with chocolate chips.

5 Minute Microwave Cornbread

Prep: 7 mins

Cook: 3 mins

Total: 10 mins

Servings: 6

Ingredients

- 1/2 cup flour
- 1/2 c cornmeal
- 2 tbsp white sugar
- 2 tsp baking powder
- 1/4 tsp salt
- 1 egg
- 1/2 cup milk
- 2 tbsp vegetable oil

Directions

☐ Step 1

Prep all ingredients in a microwave-safe glass or ceramic bowl.

☐ Step 2

Microwave on high for 3 minutes, turning the bowl halfway through cooking if your microwave doesn't have a rotating tray.

Micro-Poached Salmon

YIELDS: 4

PREP TIME: 5 mins

TOTAL TIME: 13 mins

Ingredients

- 1 lemon
- 4 skinless salmon fillets
- 1/4 tsp salt
- 1/4 c. water

Directions

1. In an 8" x 8" glass baking dish, stack thin lemon slices. Salmon fillets on lemon slices Add salt. Fill dish with water.

2. Microwave on High for 8 minutes, or until fish is opaque throughout. Transfer salmon to paper towels to drain. 15 minutes to cool.

Single-Serve Chocolate Mug Cake

Prep: 5 minutes

Cook: 2 minutes

Total: 7 minutes

YIELD 1 SERVING

INGREDIENTS

Chocolate Mug Cake

- 1 tsp white whole wheat
- 1 tsp cocoa powder
- 1/4 tsp baking powder
- 2 tsp coconut sugar
- 1 big egg
- 1 tbsp maple syrup
- 1 tbsp milk (any kind)
- 1 tsp melted coconut or butter
- 1 tbsp tiny chocolate

Frosting

- 1 tbsp drippy nut butter
- 2 tsp cocoa powder
- 1 tsp maple syrup

INSTRUCTIONS

1. Prepare a big mug or a small dish with cooking spray.

2. In a cup, mix all mug cake ingredients and stir well.

3. Microwave on high for 60-90 seconds OR Bake at 350°F for 22-24 minutes or until thoroughly done.

4. Make the chocolate icing while the mug cake bakes. Mix in the nut butter, cocoa powder, and maple syrup. If it's too thick, add more melted coconut oil.

5. Remove the mug cake from the microwave/oven and ice it. Enjoy!

Poached Pears with Ruby-Red Raspberry Sauce

YIELDS: 2

COOK TIME: 5 mins

TOTAL TIME: 30 mins

Ingredients

- 2 Bosc pears
- 1/2 lemon
- 2 tsp sugar
- 1 1/2 c. raspberries, fresh or frozen (reserve 10 raspberries for garnish)
- 1c. icing
- 1 tbsp. liquor (black currant or orange)
- Garnish mint sprigs

Directions

1. Core pears using an apple corer or a tiny knife. Almost peel pears but leave stems on. Sugared pears with a lemon half.

2. In a glass pie dish, lay pears with stems toward the middle. Microwave uncovered on High for 5-6 minutes, rotating pears halfway through. Place pears on 2 dessert dishes, stems up, and leave aside until serving.

3. Blend raspberries at high speed. Sift confectioners' sugar into small basin. Same sieve, same bowl for raspberry purée. Toss seeds. Mix in liqueur.

4. Serve raspberry sauce with poached pears. Garnish with mint and raspberries.

Microwave Mug Chocolate Cake

YIELDS:1 serving

TOTAL TIME: 8 mins

INGREDIENTS

- 1 tbsp unsalted buter
- Chopped bittersweet chocolate 2 ounces
- 1 big egg
- 2 tsp sugar (brown)
- 1 1/2 tsp. vanilla
- 2 tsp Flour
- 2 tsp cocoa powder
- 1/2 tsp. baking powder
- kosher salt
- whipped cream or topping

DIRECTIONS

1. Microwave the butter and chocolate for 20 seconds at a time until smooth; cool for 5 minutes.

2. Mix in the egg, sugar, and vanilla. Then add the flour and salt. Microwave on high for 90 seconds or until slightly underbaked. If desired, top with whipped cream.

Microwave Oatmeal Bars

Total Time Prep: 20 min.

Makes 15 servings

Ingredients

- 2 cup quick cook oats
- 1/2 cup packed sugar
- 1/2 c melted butter
- 1/4 c corn syrup
- 1 cup sweet chocolate chips

Directions

1. Combine oats and brown sugar. Add butter and syrup. Preparation: Grease a 9-in.
2. uncovered for 1-1/2 minutes on high. Stir in half a turn; microwave 1.5 minutes. Add chocolate chips. For 4-1/2 minutes at 30% power, until chips are shiny; spread chocolate evenly.
3. Refrigerate for 15-20 minutes.

Honey-Lemon Chicken Enchiladas

Total Time: 30 min.

Makes 6 servings

Ingredients

- 1 cup honey
- 2 tbsp lemon or lime
- 1 tsp canola oil

- 2 tsp chili powder
- 1/4 t garlic powder
- 3 CUP shredded COOKED CHICK
- 2 cans (10 ounces each) enchilada verde
- 12 heated corn tortillas (6 inch)
- 3/4 cup shredded low-fat cheddar
- Optional sliced green onions and tomatoes

Directions

1. In a big basin, mix the first five. Toss in the chicken.

2. Pour 1 enchilada sauce can into a greased 11x7-in. 1/4 cup chicken mixture each tortilla, off-center. Place seam side down in prepared dish. Finish with enchilada sauce.

3. Microwave on high for 11-13 minutes, covered. Add cheese. Add green onions and tomatoes to taste.

15-Minute Meat Loaf

Total Time : 15 min.

Makes 4 servings

Ingredients

- 1 big gently beaten egg
- 5 tbsp ketchup
- 2 tsp prepared mustard
- 1/2 CUP DRY bread
- 2 tbsp onion soup mix
- 1/4 tsp salt
- 1/4 tsp pepper
- 1 lb. ground beef
- 1/4 c sugar

- 2 tbsp brown sugar
- 2 tbsp cider vinegar

Directions

1. Toss the egg with the 2 tablespoons ketchup, mustard, bread crumbs and dry soup mix in a large bowl. Mix in beef crumbles. Form an oval loaf.
2. Microwave in a small 1-qt. dish. Microwave covered for 10-12 minutes on high until no pink remains and a thermometer reaches 160°; drain.
3. Drizzle with sugar, vinegar, and leftover ketchup. Microwave covered on high for 2-3 minutes. 10 minutes before slicing

Fruit & Granola Crisp with Yogurt

Total Time : 10 min.

Makes 4 servings

Ingredients

- 3 cups sliced peaches, thawed
- 1 cup thawed blueberries
- 4 tbsp hot caramel ice cream
- 4 tbsp granola without raisins
- 2 cup frozen yogurt

Directions

8 oz. ramekins with peaches and blueberries Caramel and granola on top. Microwave uncovered on high for 1-2 minutes. a spoonful of frozen yogurt

Microwave Egg Sandwich

Total Time : 15 min.

Makes 1 serving

Ingredients

- 1 piece bacon
- 1/4 cup egg substitute
- 1 tbsp salsa
- 1 tsp shredded cheddar cheese
- 1 toasted whole wheat English muffin
- 3 spinach leaves

Directions

1. Coat a 6-oz. ramekin or custard cup with cooking spray. Top with egg replacement. Microwave on high for 30 seconds, stirring. Microwave for 15-30 seconds or until almost set. Top with salsa and cheese. Microwave cheese for 10 seconds.

2. Fill English muffin with spinach. Replace English muffin top with egg and bacon.

Zucchini Ham Frittata

Total Time : 25 min.

Makes 4 servings

Ingredients

- 4 cup sliced zucchini (3-4 medium)
- 1 chopped onion
- 4 big eggs
- 3/4 tsp salt
- 1/8 t pepper
- 1 cup grated cheddar cheese
- 1 cup cooked ham cubes

Directions

1. Combine zucchini and onion in a 9-in. 3-4 minutes on high, covered, until tender; drain.

2. In a bowl, combine eggs, salt, and pepper. Pour over zucchini mix. Take out of the microwave and let cool for a few minutes before serving.

Microwaved Parmesan Chicken

Total Time: 10 min.

Makes 2 servings

Ingredients

- 2 chicken breast halves, skinless (4 ounces each)
- 4 tsp low-sodium soy sauce
- 1/4 t garlic powder
- 1/8 t pepper
- 1/4 cup grated Parmesan cheese
- 1 tbsp butter

Directions

Preheat microwave and prepare chicken. Simmer for 5 minutes. Cheese and butter sprinkling Uncover and cook on high for 4–5 minutes, or until 170°.

Cod Delight

Total Time: 15 min.

Makes 4 servings

Ingredients

- 1 tomato, chopped
- 1/3 cup onion
- 2 tbsp water
- 2 tbsp canola oil

- 4–5 tsp lemon juice
- 1 tsp dried parsley
- 1/2 t basil dried basil
- 1 minced garlic clove
- 1/8 t salt
- 4 calf fillets (4 ounces each)
- 1 tsp fish seasoning

Directions

Mix the first nine ingredients in a bowl. Top fish with tomato mixture in 11x7 baking dish. Add seafood seasoning. Microwave on high for 5-6 minutes, covered, until salmon flakes readily with a fork.

Dressed-Up Meatballs

Total Time: 20 min.

Makes 8 servings

Ingredients

- 2-pound frozen homestyle meatballs, thawed
- 2 julienned medium carrots
- 1 small onion, cut
- 1 julienned green pepper
- 1 minced garlic clove
- 1 jar (10 ounces) sour sauce
- 4-1/2 tsp soy sauce
- Hot rice

Directions

1. Place meatballs in a 3-qt. microwave-safe dish. Pour sweet-and-sour sauce over meatballs.

2. 2-4 minutes in the microwave covered on high until veggies are soft and meatballs are cooked thoroughly. With rice.

Breakfast Potatoes

Total Time: 15 min.

Makes2 servings

Ingredients

- Peel and slice 2 medium potatoes
- 1/4 c chopped onion
- 1/4 t salt
- 1/8 t pepper
- 1/4 tsp. garlic
- 1/4 cup cheddar shredded

Directions

Spray a 9-in. microwave-safe dish. Plate potato and onion slices with spices. Tenderize potatoes in the microwave for 9-10 minutes, adding cheese in the last 30 seconds.

Sandwiches with Mashed Potatoes

Total Time: 10 min.

Makes 4 servings

Ingredients

- 1 lb sliced deli beef
- 2 cans (10-1/4 oz.) beef gravy
- drained mushroom stem can 4 oz
- 1 pkg (3 3/4 oz) buttery immediately mashed
- 4 x 1/2 inch thick Italian bread

Directions

1. Combine the meat, gravy, and mushrooms in a 2-qt. Microwave covered for 2-3 minutes on high until warm.

2. Meanwhile, prepare potatoes as directed. 4 plates of bread Pour meat over bread. With potatoes

Salmon with Tarragon Sauce

Total Time: 20 min.

Makes 4 servings

Ingredients

- 1 salmon filet (6 ounces each)
- 1/4 tsp salt
- 1/4 tsp salt
- 2 tbsp white wine or broth
- 1 tbsp butter
- 1 green onion, chopped
- 1 tsp all-purpose flour
- 1 tsp Dijon
- 1/2 t dried tarragon
- 2/3 cup 2% milk

Directions

1. Salt and pepper fish in a greased 2-qt. microwave-safe dish. Add wine on top. Microwave covered on high for 4-6 minutes or until salmon flakes easily. Remove and warm salmon.

2. Microwave the pan juices for 1 minute with the butter and onion. Mix in the flour, mustard, and tarragon, then the milk. Pour in the hot water and whisk for 30 seconds. With salmon.

Minted Beet Salad

Total Time Prep: 20 min.

Cook: 15 min.

Makes 6 servings

Ingredients

- 5 fresh medium beets (about 2 pounds)
- 2 tbsp water
- 2 tbsp champagne vinegar
- 2 tbsp olive oil
- 1/2 t salt
- 1/4 tsp coarse pepper
- 1/4 cup quartered kalamata olives
- 2 tbsp fresh mint, chopped

Directions

1. Trim beets to 1 in. Place in a large microwave-safe dish. Water drizzling Microwave covered on high for 14-15 minutes, rotating once; let stand 5 minutes.

2. Peel and cut beets into 3/4-in. pieces when cold. Whisk vinegar, oil, salt, and pepper in a basin. Toss in olives, beets, and 1 tablespoon mint. Refrigerate covered for 1 hour. 1 tablespoon mint on top

Coconut Acorn Squash

Total Time: 20 min.

Makes 4 servings

Ingredients

- 2 acorn squash
- 1/4 c. mango chutney

- 1/4 cup shredded coconut
- 3 tbsp melted butter
- 1 tsp salt
- 1/8 t pepper

Directions

1. Halve each squash and remove the seeds. Prepare a microwave-safe dish. Microwave on high for 10-12 minutes, covered.

2. Cut side up. Fill squash with chutney, coconut, and melted butter. Add salt and pepper. Microwave covered for 2-3 minutes.

Microwave Beef & Cheese Enchiladas

Total Time : 25 min.

Makes 3 servings

Ingredients

- 1/2 lb. ground beef
- 2 tsp onion
- 2 cups shredded cheddar cheese, divided
- 1 enchilada sauce can (10 oz)
- 1 tbsp chopped green chilies
- 6 warm corn tortillas
- Optional lettuce and sour cream

Directions

1. a 2-qt. microwave-safe dish with meat and onion. Microwave covered on high for 2-3 minutes; drain. 1/4 cup enchilada sauce and green chiles
2. Spread 1/2 cup beef mixture on each tortilla. Place seam-side down in a greased 11x7-in. microwave-safe dish. Finish with enchilada sauce.

3. Microwave covered on high for 5-6 minutes. Rest of cheese on top. Cook uncovered for 1-2 minutes more to melt cheese. Optional lettuce and sour cream

Quick Poached Salmon with Cucumber Sauce

Total Time: 20 min.

Makes 4 servings

Ingredients

- 1 c water
- 1/2 small onion, cut
- Parsley 1 sprigs
- 1/4 tsp salt
- 5 Peppercorns
- 4 sockeye fillet (6 ounces each)

sauce:

- 1/2 c sour cream
- 1/3 Cucumber, diced, seeded
- 1 tbsp chopped onion
- 1/4 tsp salt
- 1/4 t basil dried

Directions

1. In an 11x7-inch microwave-safe dish, mix the first six ingredients. Microwave uncovered on high for 2-3 minutes until mixture boils.

2. Carefully add salmon. 5-1/2 minutes, covered, at 70% power, until salmon flakes readily with a fork.

1. Preheat oven to 350°F. 2. Medium heat oil in a big skillet. Discard poaching liquid. With sauce.

Microwaved Chicken Kiev

Total Time : 30 min.

Makes 4 servings

Ingredients

- 5 tbsp softened butter
- 1/2 tsp minced chives
- 1/4 t garlic powder
- 1/4 tsp white pepper
- 4 deboned skinless chicken breasts (6 ounces each)
- 1/3 cup cornflakes
- 1 tsp grated Parmesan
- 1/2 tsp dried parsley
- 1/4 tsp paprika

Directions

1. Combine 3 tablespoons butter, chives, garlic powder, and pepper in a small bowl. Cover and freeze for 10 minutes.
2. Meanwhile, flatten chicken breast halves to 1/4 in. Place a butter cube in the middle. Fold long sides over butter, then fasten with toothpick ends.
3. Combine cornflakes, cheese, parsley, and paprika. Melt butter. Coat chicken in butter, then with cornflakes. Prepare a microwave-safe dish.
4. 5-6 minutes in the microwave uncovered, until chicken juices flow clear and thermometer reaches 170°. Toenails removed Drizzle with pan drippings if you want.

Chipotle Ranch Chicken Tacos

Total Time: 20 min.

Makes 4 servings

Ingredients

- 2 cups shredded rotisserie chicken
- 2 cups thawed frozen corn
- ¼ cup pico de
- 8 taco shells (warm)
- 1 cup Monterey Jack cheese shredded
- 1 cup cole slaw
- 6 radishes, cut
- 2 tbsp chipotle ranch
- 3 Jalapenos, seeded and sliced

Directions

1. Microwave the chicken, corn, and pico de gallo together. Cover and heat on high for 1-2 minutes.
2. Taco shells with chicken combination Rest of ingredients on top

Italian Chicken Cordon Bleu

Total Time: 30 min.

Makes 6 servings

Ingredients

- 2 tbsp cubed butter
- 1/2 tsp rubbed sage
- 6 boneless skinless chicken breast (4 ounces each)
- 1 green pepper, julienned
- 1/3 cup fresh mushroom slices
- 1 (15 oz) tomato sauce
- 1 tsp sugar
- 1 tsp oregano
- 1/2 t salt 10. 1/2 t garlic powder
- 1 tsp lemon pepper seasoning
- 6 Swiss cheese slices

- Optional hot cooked rice

Directions

1. Microwave butter and sage in an 11x7-in. Allow to stand for 30 seconds or until butter has melted. Turn chicken in dish to coat. Add mushrooms and green pepper. Cook uncovered on high for 8-10 minutes, flipping and rearranging chicken twice.

1. Preheat oven to 375°F 2. Mix in tomato sauce, sugar, and spices. Microwave uncovered for 2 minutes on high or until warm. Replenish with ham, cheese, and green pepper combination. 2 minutes on high until cheese melts. Optional rice served.

Mini Burgers with the Works

Total Time: 30 min.

Makes 1 dozen

Ingredients

- 1/4 lb. ground beef
- 3 sliced American
- 4 white bread (heels of loaves recommended)
- 2 tbsp Thousand Island salad dressing
- 2 pearl onions, sliced
- 4 sliced baby dill pickles
- 3 sliced cherry tomatoes

Directions

1. Form meat into 12 1in patties. Microwave on a paper towel-lined plate. 1 minute on high or until meat is no longer pink. Set aside four cheese slices each.

2. From each piece of bread, cut 6 circles with a 1-in. Dress half the bread circles. Compose with burgers and cheese. Rest of bread circles on top; toothpicks fasten.

Super-Stuffed Mexican Potatoes

Total Time: 25 min

Makes 4 servings

Ingredients

- 4 big Baked Potatoes
- 1 jars black bean and corn salsa
- 6 oz. Grilled chicken breast strips
- 1 CUP PROCESS CHEESE (Velveeta)
- 1 chopped tomato
- Toppings: sour cream, green onions, and sliced ripe olives

Directions

1. Prep potatoes by washing and piercing them. 15-17 minutes, uncovered, on high, rotating once.
2. Meanwhile, mix the salsa, chicken, and cheese. Stir until cheese is melted.
3. Score each potato with a "X" and fluff with a fork. Sprinkle with tomato and salsa mixture. Choose your own toppings.

Turkey Enchilada Stack

Total Time: 20 min.

Makes 4 servings

Ingredients

- 1 lb lean turkey
- 2 low-salt tomato sauce cans (8 oz.)
- 3 tsp minced onion
- 1/2 tsp garlic powder
- 1/2 tsp pepper
- 1/4 tsp salt

- 4 wheat tortillas (8 inches)
- 2/3 cup shredded low-fat cheddar
- Toppings: lettuce, tomatoes, and low-fat sour cream

Directions

1. Cook until no longer pink; drain. Heat through tomato sauce, chopped onion, garlic powder, pepper, and salt.

2. In a 2-1/2-qt. microwave-safe circular dish, put 1 tortilla, 3/4 cup meat mixture, and 3 tablespoons cheese. 3 layers total Microwave on high for 4-5 minutes, covered. Wait 5 minutes before cutting. If desired, add toppings.

Granola Cereal Bars

Total Time Prep: 15 min

Makes 1 dozen

Ingredients

- 1/2 cup brown sugar
- 1/2 CUP peanut butter
- 1/2 cup corn syrup
- 1 tsp vanilla
- 2 cups oats
- 1 1/2 CUP CRISP RICE
- 1/4 cup mini-chocolates chips

Directions

Microwave the brown sugar, peanut butter, and corn syrup on high for 2 minutes, stirring once. Add vanilla, oats, and cereal. Chocolaty chips Fill a 9-inch square pan with batter. Cool and slice.

Chicken and Rice Soup Mix

Total Time: 10 min.

Makes 1 serving

Ingredients

- Uncooked instant rice, 2 tbsp
- 1 1/2 tsp reduced-sodium chicken bouillon
- 1 tsp celery flakes
- 1 tsp dried parsley flakes
- 1/4 tsp minced onion
- 1/8 t pepper

additional ingredients:

- 3/4 cup boiled water
- 1 c. (5 oz.) chunk white

Directions

1. Combine the first six ingredients. Move to a spice jar. Keep cold and dry for 6 months. 4 tbsp

2. To make soup: Soup mix in a microwave-safe bowl. Soak for 5 minutes in boiling water. Add chicken. Heating on high for 1-2 minutes, uncovered.

Bart's Black Bean Soup for Two

Total Time: 10 min.

Makes 2 servings

Ingredients

- 3/4 cup washed and drained black beans
- 3/4 c. Chicken broth
- 1/3 cup salsa
- 1/4 cup corn kernels
- Dash hot sauce
- 1 tsp lime juice

- 1/2 cup cheddar cheese
- 1 tsp green onion

Directions

Mix first five ingredients in a microwave-safe bowl. Microwave covered for 2 minutes on high until warm. Pour into two serving dishes and lime juice each. Cheese and green onions

Instant Mac & Cheese in a Mug

Prep Time5 minutes

Total Time5 minutes

Yield1 serving

Ingredients

- 1/3 cup uncooked tiny macaroni elbow noodles
- 1/2 cup water
- 1/4 cup milk
- 1/2 cup finely shredded cheese (we prefer cheddar/jack)

Instructions

1. In a cup combine macaroni and water. Cook on high for 2 minutes. Stir. (Note: if the water boils slightly, that is OK.)
2. Microwave for 1 minute. Stir.
3. Microwave for a fourth minute, then verify for complete absorption. If not, microwave until gone.
4. Microwave for 30-60 seconds with the milk and cheese. Enjoy a good stir.

Quick Egg, Mushroom & Ham Cup

Prep Time: 5 minutes

Cook Time: 3 minutes

Total Time: 8 minutes

Ingredients

- 4 eggs
- 4 tbsp water
- 2/3 cup finely diced shiitake
- 3 deli ham slices sliced (about 3 ounces)
- 1/4 tsp freshly ground black
- 2 tbsp grated cheddar

Instructions

1. spray 2 12-ounce microwave-safe coffee cups
2. In each cup, crack 2 eggs and whisk in 2 tbsp water.
3. Divide the mushrooms, ham, and pepper into the two cups.
4. Microwave the cups for 60 seconds on HIGH.
5. Microwave the mixture in each mug for 60-90 seconds until almost set.
6. Garnish with cheese and serve.

EGG FRIED RICE IN A MUG

Prep Time: 5 minutes

Cook Time: 3 minutes

Total Time: 9 minutes

Yield: 1 serving 1x

INGREDIENTS

- 1 cup jasmine rice
- 2 tbsp frozen peas
- 2 tsp red pepper
- 1/2 green onion stalk, cut
- mung bean shoots

- shredded purple cabbage
- 1 big egg
- 1 tsp soy sauce
- 1/2 tsp sesame oil
- 1/2 tsp onion powder
- 1/4 tsp five-spice powder

INSTRUCTIONS

1. Put the rice in a big cup. Atop that, put the peas and red peppers and green onions. Cling film the cup. Puncture the film with a knife. This is vital! You don't want to scald. Microwave on high for 1:15.

2. Meanwhile, beat the egg and spices (soy sauce, sesame oil, onion powder and five-spice powder). Mix the egg mixture with the veggies and rice in the cup.

3. Microwave for 1 minute 15 seconds to 1 minute 30 seconds, covered with cling film. Remove the cup from the microwave and stir well. Allow the fried rice to cool for a minute. Serve the rice with a fork.

1-minute Microwave Quiche in a Mug

Total time: 3 minutes
Prep time: 2 min
Cook time: 1 min
Yield: 1 serving

Ingredients:

- 1 big egg
- 1 1/2 tsp milk (substitutes: half and half or heavy cream)
- 1 tsp unsalted butter
- 1 tsp salt

- freshly ground black
- 4 halved grape tomatoes
- 1/8 cup fresh bread ripped
- 1 tbsp grated (e.g., cheddar cheese, mozzarella, etc.)
- 1 tsp chopped fresh herbs

Directions:

1. In a microwaveable cup, combine egg, milk, melted butter, salt, and pepper. Add half grape tomatoes, broken bread, grated cheese, and chopped herbs on top of egg mixture, mixing well. Ingredients will remain better in the quiche recipe if you don't stir them in.

2. Microwave for 1 minute on high, or until egg is fully cooked and quiche is slightly puffed. Serve immediately with fresh herbs.

Homemade Single-Serve Microwave Spaghetti

Prep Time 5 minutes

Cook Time 10 minutes

Total Time 15 minutes

Ingredients

- 1/3 cup salad macaroni
- 1/3+1/4 cup water
- 2 1/2 tbsp tomato spaghetti sauce I prefer the garlic one.
- 1/4 c. shredded colby jack cheese

Instructions

Microwave macaroni and water in a large dish or cup (I use a big soup mug). 7 minutes, stopping to stir at: 5, 4, 2, 1, 30 sec. Heat sauce and cheese in the microwave. a 30 second microwave Remove from microwave, mix, and serve.

SPINACH RICOTTA LASAGNA IN A MUG

Serves 1

Prep Time: 12 minutes

Cook Time: 3 minutes

Total Time: 15 minutes

INGREDIENTS

- 2 new lasagna sheets
- 2 1/2 cups (75g) baby spinach
- 1/4 tbsp sliced yellow bell
- 1/4 cup ricotta cheese
- 3 big finely chopped basil leaves (optional)
- 1/4 tsp salt
- 1/8 granulated garlic
- 6 tbsp spaghetti sauce
- 1/3 cup part-skim mozzarella shreds

INSTRUCTIONS

1. Cut each lasagna strip in half. Pour boiling water over the spaghetti sheets until they are completely covered. My electric kettle boiled boiling water. Set aside the pasta.
2. Place spinach in microwave-safe bowl and chop. Cover the top with plastic wrap and make ventilation holes. 1 min. in microwave Remove the spinach and rest.
3. While the spinach cools, grated the mozzarella.
4. Combine spinach, ricotta, pepper, garlic, and salt. Set aside.
5. Put 2 tablespoons spaghetti sauce in the cup. Add a softened spaghetti sheet on top. 2 tbsp mozzarella, and a pasta sheet Continue layering the lasagna, finishing with a pasta sheet on top. Add mozzarella to spaghetti.
6. Microwave for 1 min 30 sec. Ensure the mozzarella is melted. Microwave at 15-second intervals until the cheese is melted.
7. Serve right away.

PIZZA MUG CAKE

Servings: 1

prep time: 4 minutes

Cook time: 1 minute

Total time: 5 minutes

INGREDIENTS

- 4 tsp flour
- 1/8 tsp baking powder
- 1/16Tsp Baking Sod
- 1/8 tsp salt
- Italian seasoning, 1/2 tsp
- 3 tsp fat-free milk
- 1 tbsp vegetable oil
- 1 tbsp shredded mozzarella
- 14 pepperoni mini
- side marinara sauce

INSTRUCTIONS

1. Then add the milk and oil with a little whisk. Use a microwave-safe cup or 6-oz ramekin. If using ramekins, whisk carefully, adding flour gradually. Mix until smooth.
2. Mix with 1 tbsp shredded cheese and 7 tiny pepperoni. 1 tbsp cheese over batter Top with remaining tiny pepperoni. Microwave for 1 minute. with marinara (either drizzle on top, or dip in spoonfuls).

Hasty Chocolate Pudding

Prep: 5 mins

Cook: 10 mins

Total: 15 mins

Servings: 4

Yield: 4 servings

Ingredients

- 1/2 cup sugar
- 1/3 c unsweetened cocoa
- 3 tbsp cornstarch
- 2 c milk
- 2 tsp vanilla

Directions

☐ Step 1

Sugar, cocoa, and cornstarch in a microwave-safe dish. Whisk in milk gradually to avoid dry lumps.

☐ Step 2

Microwave for 3 minutes on high. Cook for 1 minute at a time, stirring every 2–4 minutes, until glossy and thick. Add vanilla.

☐ Step 3

Refrigerate the pudding with a plastic wrap immediately on top to prevent a skin from developing. Cool.

Potato Chips

Prep: 30 mins

Cook: 5 mins

Total: 35 mins

Servings: 4

Ingredients

- 1 tbsp vegetable oil
- 1 paper-thin potato (peel optional)
- 1/2 teaspoon salt

Directions

☐ Step 1

Put the oil in a plastic bag (a produce bag works well). Shake in the potato slices.

☐ Step 2

Lightly oil or spray a large dinner dish. Lay down the potato pieces in a single layer.

☐ Step 3

3–5 minutes in the microwave until gently browned (if not browned, they will not become crisp). The time depends on the microwave's power. Toss salty chips on dish (or other seasonings). Cool. Rep with remaining potato slices. You won't need to oil the plate.

Microwave Baked Potato

Prep: 1 min

Cook: 11 mins

Total: 12 mins

Servings: 1

Yield: 1 serving

Ingredients

- 1 big russet
- 1 tbsp butter
- 3 tsp grated Cheddar cheese
- a dash of salt & pepper
- 3 sour cream

Directions

☐ Step 1

Scrub the potato and puncture it with a fork. On a platter.

☐ Step 2

Microwave on high power for 5 minutes. Cook for 5 minutes more. Remove from microwave when soft and cut in half lengthwise. Salt, pepper, and mash with a fork. Butter and 2 tablespoons cheese on the open sides Return to microwave for 1 minute to melt cheese.

☐ Step 3

Serve with leftover cheese and sour cream.

Chili Cheese Dip V

Prep: 10 mins

Cook: 5 mins

Total: 15 mins

Servings: 32

Yield: 4 cups

Ingredients

- 1 package softened cream cheese
- 15 oz. chili
- 1 cup grated Cheddar

Directions

☐ Step 1

Butter a 9-inch round microwave-safe baking dish. Stack chili on top of cream cheese. Cheese the chili with Cheddar.

☐ Step 2

5 minutes on high until cheese melts.

Southwest Chicken Casserole

Servings: 4

Yield: 4 servings

Ingredients

- 1 5 oz. drained chicken pieces
- 1 (4 oz) chopped green chilies
- 1 can (10.75 oz) condensed mushroom soup
- 2 cups shredded Cheddar
- 2 tbsp dried minced onion
- salt and pepper
- 1 1/4 cup water
- 2 c instant rice

Directions

☐ Step 1

A 9x13 inch microwave safe casserole dish with chicken chiles soup cheese onions salt pepper and water

☐ Step 2

Add rice. It should be like a soupy pancake batter.

☐ Step 3

Microwave for 15 minutes with a cover or plastic wrap on the dish (depending on the microwave). If desired, add maxi corn and green salad.

Microwave Oven Peanut Brittle

Prep: 10 mins

Cook: 20 mins

Total: 30 mins

Servings: 16

Yield: 1 pound

Ingredients

- 1 1/2 cup dry rotten peanuts
- 1 cup sugar
- 1/2 c light corn syrup
- 1 t salt (optional)
- 1 tbsp butter
- 1 tsp vanilla
- 1 t baking soda

Directions

☐ Step 1

Prep a baking sheet with butter. Peanuts, sugar, corn syrup, and salt Microwave on High (700 W) for 6–7 minutes until bubbling and peanuts are browned. Cook 2–3 minutes longer with butter and vanilla.

☐ Step 2

Stir in baking soda until frothy. Fill into oiled baking sheet. Allow to cool for 15 minutes. Break into pieces and keep tightly.

Shelby's Microwave Meat Loaf

Prep: 20 mins

Cook: 15 mins

Additional: 10 mins

Total: 45 mins

Servings: 6

Ingredients

- 1 (8 oz) tomato sauce
- 1/4 c brown sugar
- 1 tsp. prepared mustard
- 2 gently beaten eggs
- 1 minced onion
- 1/4 c green bell pepper mince
- 1/4 tsp garlic powder
- 1/2 cup saltine crumbs
- 1 tsp salt
- 1/4 tsp black pepper
- 2 lb. extra lean beef

Directions

☐ Step 1

Mix tomato sauce, brown sugar, and mustard.

☑ Step 2

Onion and green pepper minced; ground beef and half of the tomato sauce mixture mixed until the meat loaf is well blended. Into a 2-quart microwave-safe baking dish. Length of time: 30 min.

☐ Step 3

Microwave on High for 10–15 minutes, until set, fluids flow clear, and meat is no longer pink inside. A meat thermometer placed into the loaf should read 165°F (75 degrees C). Leave exposed for 10–15 minutes.

Microwave Loin of Pork

Prep: 10 mins

Cook: 22 mins

Total: 32 mins

Servings: 3

Ingredients

- 2 lb boneless pork loin
- 2 tbsp fresh rosemary chopped
- 1/2 cup water
- 3 onions, halved
- 1 tsp salt
- 1 tsp black pepper
- 1 tsp dried thyme
- 1 tsp cumin

Directions

☐ Step 1

Dry the pork roast and perforate it with a knife or fork at 1 inch intervals. Insert rosemary leaves in holes.

☐ Step 2

Fill a 9 or 10 inch pie dish with onion halves. Use the onions as a roasting rack for the meat. Season the meat with salt, pepper, thyme, and cumin.

☐ Step 3

Microwave on high for 16 minutes (or about 8 minutes per pound). Cook for 6 minutes more on the other side, or until the roast reaches 145°F (63 degrees C). Allow 15 minutes resting time before cutting and serving.

Basic Microwave Risotto

Servings: 4

Yield: 4 servings

Ingredients

- 3 tbsp butter
- 1 minced garlic clove
- 1 chopped onion
- 1 1/2 c vegetable broth
- 1 cup Arborio rice
- 3/4 wine white
- 1/4 c grated Parmesan

Directions

☐ Step 1

a 3 quart microwave-safe casserole dish Microwave for 3 minutes on high.

☐ Step 2

Microwave safe dish with vegetable broth Microwave until heated but not boiling (approximately 2 minutes).

☐ Step 3

Pour the rice and broth over the onion, butter, and garlic combination. Cook on high for 6 minutes, closely covered.

☐ Step 4

Pour wine over rice. Cook for 10 minutes on high. Most liquid should evaporate. Serve the rice with cheese.

Gourmet Microwave Popcorn

Prep: 5 mins

Cook: 5 mins

Total: 10 mins

Servings: 2

Yield: 2 cups

Ingredients

- 1/4 unpopped cup popcorn
- a dash salt
- 1 tsp olive oil

Directions

☐ Step 1

Put popcorn in a bag. Finish by folding the top many times.

☐ Step 2

Stir well and microwave on high for 2 minutes. Open the bag gently. Salt and olive oil to taste. Shake the spice bag to mix.

Microwave Chocolate Mug Cake

Prep: 5 mins

Cook: 2 mins

Total: 7 mins

Servings: 1

Yield: 1 cake

Ingredients

- 1/4 cup flour
- 1/4 c white sugar
- 2 tsp unsweetened cocoa powder
- 1/8 tsp baking soda
- 1/8 tsp salt
- 3 tsp milk
- 2 tbsp canola oil
- 1 tbsp water
- 1/4 tsp vanilla

Directions

☐ Step 1

In a large microwave-safe cup, combine flour, sugar, cocoa powder, baking soda, and salt.

☐ Step 2

In 1 minute 45 seconds, microwave

Microwave Corn on the Cob

Cook: 5 mins

Total: 5 mins

Servings: 1

Yield: 1 serving

Ingredients

1 husked and cleaned corn

Directions

☐ Step 1

Wring out a paper towel. Place the wet ear of corn on a dinner dish. Microwave for 5 minutes. Remove the paper towel and enjoy!

Printed in Great Britain
by Amazon